This edition published in the United States of America in 2012 by Universe Publishing,
A Division of Rizzoli International Publications, Inc.
300 Park Avenue South New York, NY 10010
www.rizzoliusa.com

2012 2013 2014 2015 / 10 9 8 7 6 5 4 3 2 1

Printed in China

ISBN: 978-0-7893-2083-4

Library of Congress Control Number: 2012932509

A POEM as BIG as NEW YORK CITY

little kids write about the big apple

Illustrated by Masha D'yans
Edited by Teachers & Writers Collaborative
Foreword by Walter Dean Myers
Adapted by Melanie Marie Goodreaux

FOReVVORD BY WALTER DEAN MYERS

The Harlem tenement I lived in offered no relief from the scorching summer heat. I was fifteen, struggling with family problems, and wondering what I would be doing with my life, when I heard about a contest for young poets. The assignment was to write, in poetic form, a portrait of New York. I took my black-and-white composition book and started writing.

At first the writing was all from my head, an exercise in putting words on paper. Then I started looking around me and, more important, I began to see and hear and smell and feel the city I had grown up in. Suddenly, the familiar became gloriously new. The fire escape I had slept on to escape my airless apartment grew into a dark, symbolic geometry that changed my point of view. As I wandered the streets, seeing people interact, hearing how the rumble of the Broadway train perfectly backed the staccato voices of children playing in the shadows beneath them, I was seeing a new city. I was also becoming a new person. I was becoming a person who saw with a constantly fresh vision, who listened more intently, whose imagination was permanently stretched.

So it is with the young poets whose work, whose images, whose cultural reweaving of the familiar is represented in A Poem as Big as New York City. Sometimes the poets show up with startling representations of the world they live in painted in a language as fresh as the city itself. At other times the poets dance between the words as they accept their roles as integral parts of the city they depict.

If anyone wants to know the reasons for bringing young people to art, they will find those reasons here. These are young people learning to celebrate the ordinary and to transform that ordinary into the rich stuff of life. They boldly discard the stale as they bring their own rich and unique inner visions to the page. I am sometimes surprised at the talent represented here, but not the creativity. It is what young people are capable of when given the chance.

I didn't win the contest as a teenager, but I did become another person, one who would spend a lifetime doing what I did, wandering the streets of New York. I was thankful for the chance to be a poet that summer and to learn from the experience of enjoying my city. I still am.

FROM MASHA D'YANS

As a New Yorker endlessly excited by the city, I was thrilled and honored to work with Teachers & Writers Collaborative on this project. But how does one illustrate a subject as big as New York City? Especially since it already inspired so many tough acts to follow … The young poets showed me a way! Their words playfully mix the surreal with the mundane, vocalizing the vibrant rhythms of the city as both the subject and the observer. Amazingly, the poem itself becomes a character through whose eyes we can take a new look at the greatest city in the world. The words liberated my artwork. My paintings strove to keep up with them; to convey the familiar as well as surprising impressions and moods of New York City rather than trying to catalog its innumerable particulars. I hope that I did justice to the children's words, I do know that they gave me a new way of looking around me, which is the great achievement for any creative pursuit. This poem is the little kid who exists within all of us, wide-eyed and craning the neck to take in as much of the wonder as possible.

FROM MELANIE MARIA GOODREAUX

The children of New York City gave me stacks of poems on hundreds of loose leaf pages to craft this unprecedented work. They scribbled lines about how big they imagined this poem to be and wrote about their love for the city in wobbling kid-created cursive—some just beginning to write within the dotted lines of handwriting paper. Many pondered how their ancestors arrived here long ago, while others noted the sights, sounds, and soul of this great city. By stringing these voices together into A Poem as Big as New York City, one child's line from Brooklyn now rhymes with another's from the Bronx. The child from Queens creates the poetic beat that bounces off the rhythm of children in Staten Island and Manhattan. Creating this poem with hundreds of New York City children was profound and delightful indeed.

When I look at the New York sky,
I see little pencils fly,
flying, flying through the sky
writing words way up high,
writing a poem of many hues
reds, oranges, greens, blues.
How did it get up there so high—
was it written by a butterfly?

Or was it a giant skipping across the New York sky,
bending over the clouds to write,
thinking a million things that you can think,
in shining sunset purple ink ...

Most see only a concrete paradise,
rough blocks, the scent of gasoline and sugared nuts,
buildings building up,
lives flying by,
planes overhead,
people below,
sirens wailing,
car horns blaring-

but there is a poem growing
from the core of this Big Apple.

A POEM AS BIG AS ...

the millions of people tuning in to watch the ball drop
when all time stops at Times Square on New Year's Eve,

A poem as big as the MAnHattAn sKyliNe viewed from the farthest ends of Brooklyn,

A POEM AS BIG AS THE CITY!

Higher than hundreds of yellow cabs on 42nd Street,

Bigger than the millions of cheese slices of New York City pizzas
going into hot, 500-degree ovens,

A poem as big as 60,000 screaming fans at a game at Yankee Stadium.

The roar of the crowd fills the neighborhood, Go, Yankees!
and wakes up angry neighbors
in the Bronx, the Bronx,

her boogie-down bright lights
protecting me from unnecessary fights,
speaking to me,
telling me it'll be all right,
and that I shouldn't give up the fight
in the Bronx, the Bronx,
a sister to me,
the Boogie-Down Bronx!

words

Fuhgeddaboudit

Mets

HAPPY NEW YEAR

Where I'm from,
there is a poem that jumps
inside a yellow cab-
zoom! WHOOSH!
ALL AROUND
New
York
City!

On top of the taxi is a flashing message for all to see:

People of the City, DREAM BIG,
dream BIGGER than a poem
that splats itself in bubble gum
across the trains
and break dances
to the pitter-patter of drums
and the bongo beats below
coming from the subway!

words words

DREAM BIG

The subway sounds
like a stampede of rhinos
and elephants underground.
The subway snake dreams

Darkity, Dark, Dark,
the subway slithers along
bumpy metallic tracks.
SPARKs!

When the subway stops at the station,
it screams with hunger,
SCRREEEEEEEECH!
The subway snake
has bolts and nails as sharp
as a wasp's stinger.
It eats up all the people, all the rats.
It doesn't chew them.
It just swallows them whole
then spits them out at another station.
The subway snake jerks to a stop,
falls fast asleep, dreams.

There is a poem that wakes up
to see the sun glistening off the Hudson River,
a poem that sees sailboats and words
gliding through the waves,
mirroring city lights,
making the sunset shimmer.

Oh, Hudson River,
I've known rivers too.
I am a river, destined to be taken away
to a deep, deep ocean.
I'll always flow, don't you know?
I am a poem as BIG as the city.

sunsetsunsetsunsetsun.
etsunsetsunsetsunsetsun:
sunsetsunsetsunset
etsunsetsunsetsuns
sunsetsunsetsunset
etsunsetsunsetsuns
sunsetsunsetsunset
etsunsetsunsetsuns
sunsetsunsetsunsel
etsunsetsunsetsun
sunsetsunsetsunse
erriverriverriv
riverriverrive
rriverriverriv
riverriverriverrive
FlowFlow
lowFLOWFl
NFLOWFlou
FlowFlowFlowFlo.
owFLOWFLOWFLOWFLOWFlowFlowFlowFlowFlowFLOWFLOWFLOWFLOWFlowFlowFlu
FLOWFLOWFLOWFLOWFl wFLOWFl FlowFLOWFLOWFLOWFLOWFlowFLOWFLOWFLOWFLOWFLOWFLOWFlou
owFLOWFLOWFLOWFlou Flowfl wFLOWFLOWFLOWFlowFLOWFLOWFLOWFLOWFLOWFLOWFlowFLOWFLc
lowFlowFLOWFlowFlo FlowFl wFLOWFLOWFlowFLOWFLOWFLOWFlowFLOWFLOWFLOWFlowFlowf
lowFlowFlowFlowFlou FLOWFlowFlowFl wFl wFl wFl owFl
NFLowFlowFlowFlc lowFlc

Hey, Statue of Liberty,
was it just me
or was it you on the A train
as big as a tree?
Now I can see
your tablet is really a MetroCard!

Oh, Statue, don't you get tired? –
Looking into their eyes,
foreseeing the crowds,
the never-ending waves,
watching the city changing
like a kaleidoscope
from day to day
never the same.

And so much depends upon
watching New York minutes
                    trickle
                        like
                            pickles ...

A flock of seagulls comes down
and offers the poem a ride.
They fly above the Verrazano Bridge,
above the blue water of New York Harbor.
The poem smells the salty seas of
                        Staten Island.

The poem rides the ferry
and hears the waves
        whoosh, whoosh,

the birds
tweet,   tweet,   and   tweet,
and the ferry
hunk, hunk.
The waves splash
and the lights flash
all the way to South Beach,
where I am scared of the jellyfish,
where I hear dogs bark
and seagulls calling their mates.

The poem went to the Aquarium
and got caught in an octopus's mouth
and swam with the sea lion.
The poem walked by the East River and reached up
to touch a pink-and-white striped sky.
It passed by the Chrysler Building,
and it looked like a wealthy woman
who just couldn't hide her jewels.

The poem bungee jumps out onto a cloud
and over the Brooklyn Bridge.

The Brooklyn Bridge bends down
like a person doing yoga,
stretching across the East River,
generously sharing its gigantic back with everyone,
its big cables gracefully coming down
like four massive harps for a giant to play.

You ever been to Brooklyn?
Don't hesitate, come to BROOKLYN.

Brooklyn is the place to be, and you know I'm right,
from Spanish to Asian, to Black and White!

So much diversity! This is who we are-
Manhattan may be the center, but Brooklyn is the star!

Let's go to the park! To Kaiser Park we go,
To hear the young people saying, "Hey, what-up, Yo."

On Coney Island,
There is a Ferris wheel that goes up, up, up and away!
How many rides can we go on today?
Cyclone! Cyclone!
        Ohhhhhh, hold on tight!

Then the poem as big as the city
turns into a moon
shaped like an elephant's big, white tusk
and it moves in a New York night as busy as a jungle.
The poem shivers like a crushed beetle in Prospect Park
and curls up into the sky like a pig's pink tail.

And then the poem glitters the road like
falling snow.

Then

d   w
    o   n

        f   l

            e   l

t   e
    h

            s   o
                n   w,

    v   e   y
           r

            s   o   f   t   l   y.

The snow looked like pearls falling from the sky,
landing on the rooftops of houses in Queens.

How snowy you are today, Elmhurst,
with all the noisy kids playing on the streets,
looking like a white blanket, snowballs flying.
You look like a bride about to be married.

How sweet you are today, Astoria.
The beautiful aroma of your scented pine trees
the guys are selling on the corner.
I love your snow, your sweet snow.

How calm you are today, College Point.
With the crack of dawn
         nothing can be heard.
            All the kids are still dreaming
                  their last dreams of the day.

How cool you are today, New York,
with all the action of Manhattan!
Your colorful wave of faces,
a place of change where everyone came—
New York, you are a bustling, LOUD, NEVER-RESTING place,
a house of mirrors,
a mastermind,

a supermodel on a runway,
a beehive,
a rocket,
a poem,
a city.

I am the city in many different ways.
I am the city on its busiest days.
I'm not powerful or loud,

breathtaking
or proud:

I come from 99-cent stores, beauty parlors, and nail salons.

I come from the smell of sea salt and the curve of carousel horse hair.

I come from honey dripping off baklava at Lefkos Pyrgos,

I come from rare steak au poivre with potatoes au gratin,
arroz con pollo with black beans, Belgian fries, bagels, shrimp lo mein,
and seared salmon with soy sauce.

I come from mangu with salami, and beans with sweets.

I come from a falafel.

I come from dark Atlantic waves and silent echoes.

I come from break-dancing in Inwood in the wind.

I come from Are you Dominican, Mexican, Boricuan, or Nuyorican?

I come from What ya gonna do is take the A train …

I am from crowded streets full of figures
with thoughts that aren't said out loud.

I am from everywhere and anywhere I call home.

And then Wepa! Wepa!

HONK! Sputt, Sputt!

VrOOOm!

Please stand clear of the

BOOM, BOOM, BOOM.
A gigantic microphone descends from the sky!

Now everyone can hear the little pencils that fly,
the pigeon wings flapping,
hands on Broadway clapping,
a stray cat napping.

Truck horns sounding like music,
the bum in the street singing,
cellular phones ringing,
a symphony playing,
an opera of car alarms,
shouting people,
shrieking subways,
blaring music,
sounds, sounds, sounds, sounds,
Uptown, Downtown, or Chinatown?

I'm jumping inside a streetlight to find the soul,
the soul of New York City.

Rap, zap, that's what I hear.
Bark, bark,
Honk, honk.

I jumped inside a parking meter
and heard the soul of New York City
crunching like quarters.

Rap, zap,
Bark, bark,
Honk, honk.

Click, Clonk, my high heels clink
as I walk down the street
with soul.

I jumped inside a boom box on Broadway
and heard the rhyming, repetitive, rowdy voice of rap,
the drums imitating city-goers' footsteps with a pitter-pat.

The music sounding,
Ba-doom! Ba-doom! Ba-doom!
My ears pounding
I ran into Carnegie Hall to hear a piano playing
traditional music, classic like cheesecake.
Is this the soul of New York City?

From there I flew into a dance club
with disco balls swirling to Rock N Roll,
shoes tapping, heels clacking, dancing,
giving New York all of their heart and soul.

CLICK

CLONK

BA-DOOM

APOLLO

SOUL TONIGHT SOUL TONIGHT

I jumped inside the subway searching for soul,
taking the people to and fro, here and there, go, go, go!

The A, B, C, and D!
The E, F, Q, and G!
The 4, 5, 6!
The 1, 2, 3!

The doors ding, dong, ding dong.
The car zip, zip, zips.
The kla-klank of the turnstiles.
The flip-flip-flop of the newspapers.

...words

...words

The du, du, du of the loud music cracking through headphones.
Ding dong, zip zip zip, kla-klank,
flip flop flip, HONK!
Ba-doom, da-dank!
Stand clear of the closing ...

All the sounds and soul combining into my brain,
the soul of the poem, the sound of the rain,

the SOUL of a POEM as BIG as the CITY,
a soul as loud as millions of voices coming into ONE,

a poem written to make people laugh and have FUN,
a poem that whispers in English, Italian, French, Spanish, Arabic, Russian,

Chinese, Japanese, and Punjabi,
a poem that sounds like YOU and ME,

a poem as BIG as the CITY.

BRONX SCHOOLS

PS/MS 004 Crotona Park West, Claremont
PS 168, Mott Haven
IS 219 New Venture School, Morrisania
PS 723, Wakefield
Academy for Scholarship and Entrepreneurship, Williamsbridge
The Forward School, Williamsbridge

BROOKLYN SCHOOLS

PS 013 Roberto Clemente, New Lots
JHS 014 Shell Bank, Sheepshead Bay
PS 154 Magnet School for Science & Technology, Windsor Terrace
PS 208 Elsa Ebeling, Farragut
JHS 223 The Montauk, Borough Park
JHS 278 Marine Park, Marine Park
PS 370, Coney Island
IS 392, Brownsville
Academy of Hospitality and Tourism, Flatbush

MANHATTAN SCHOOLS

PS 030 Hernandez/Hughes, East Harlem
JHS 054 Booker T. Washington, Manhattan Valley
PS 077 Lower Lab School, Carnegie Hill
PS 110 Florence Nightingale, Lower East Side
PS 111 Adolph S. Ochs, Clinton
PS 153 Adam Clayton Powell, Hamilton Heights
PS 178 Professor Juan Bosch, Inwood
PS/IS 187 Hudson Cliffs, Inwood
MS 247 Dual Language Middle School, Upper West Side
PS 721 Manhattan Occupational Training Center, West Village

QUEENS SCHOOLS

PS 064 Joseph P. Addabbo, Woodhaven
PS 075 Robert E. Peary, Ridgewood
PS 092 Harry T. Stewart, Corona
PS 122 Mamie Fay, Ditmars
PS 177 Robin Sue Ward, Fresh Meadows
PS 224, Glen Oaks
IS 227 Louis Armstrong, East Elmhurst
VOYAGES Preparatory, Elmhurst
World Journalism Preparatory, Flushing

STATEN ISLAND SCHOOL

PS 039 Francis J. Murphy Jr., Concord

COMMUNITY PARTNERS

Flatbush Development Corporation, Flatbush, Brooklyn
Groundswell, Washington Heights, Manhattan
Historic Richmond Town, Great Kills, Staten Island
New York Transit Museum, Cobble Hill, Brooklyn
Staten Island Museum, St. George, Staten Island
University Settlement, Lower East Side, Manhattan

A Poem as Big as New York City is a project of Teachers & Writers Collaborative (T&W). Founded in 1967, T&W seeks to educate the imagination by offering innovative creative writing programs for students and teachers, and by providing a variety of resources to support learning through the literary arts.

T&W carries out its mission by placing professional writers in New York City area schools and community sites to lead creative writing programs for young people and professional development workshops for teachers. T&W's resources on the teaching of writing include the award-winning quarterly *Teachers & Writers Magazine*.

The guiding vision for A Poem as Big as New York City was developed by Melanie Maria Goodreaux, an award-winning poet and playwright who has taught for T&W since 2001. The project began with writing workshops at sites throughout New York City, in which thousands of young people penned poetic visions of our metropolis.

BROOKLYN
PUBLIC LIBRARY
Brooklyn Central Library
Eastern Parkway Branch
Homecrest Branch
New Utrecht Branch
Saratoga Branch

NEW YORK
PUBLIC LIBRARY
Bloomingdale Branch
Bronx Library Center
Columbus Branch
Grand Concourse Branch
Hunt's Point Branch
96th Street Branch
115th Street Branch

QUEENS
PUBLIC LIBRARY
Cambria Heights Branch
Far Rockaway Branch
Hollis Branch
Howard Beach Branch
Queens Village Branch
South Jamaica Branch

Agnes Gund
Amazon.com
Axe-Houghton Foundation
Barnes & Noble
Bloomberg Philanthropies
Bydale Foundation
Carnegie Corporation of New York
Cerimon Fund
Con Edison
The E.H.A. Foundation
ING Financial Services
JPMorgan Chase/Washington Mutual Bank Foundation
LEGO Children's Fund
Lily Auchincloss Foundation
The Lotos Foundation
Mayor Michael Bloomberg
National Endowment for the Arts
New York City Council
New York City Department of Cultural Affairs
New York City Department of Education
New York Daily News
New York State Council on the Arts
Rizzoli New York
Scheide Fund
Simon & Eve Colin Foundation
Smith Barney (Citigroup Foundation)
Wells Fargo
William Randolph Hearst Foundation

TEACHERS & WRITERS COLLABORATIVE GRATEFULLY ACKNOWLEDGES
SUPPORTERS OF T&W CREATIVE WRITING PROGRAMS,
RESOURCES FOR WRITING TEACHERS, AND A POEM AS BIG AS NEW YORK CITY.

T&W is grateful to the writers who led these workshops, to our community partners and
funders, and to Melanie for adapting the work of young New York poets to create
A Poem as Big as New York City. Special thanks also to Walter Dean Myers, Masha D'yans,
Craig Hensala, and Robb Pearlman.

To learn more about Teachers & Writers Collaborative and our programs for school children in New
York City and surrounding areas, visit www.twc.org or contact info@twc.org.

A Poem as Big as New York City was born in the imagination and creativity of young people
throughout the city's five boroughs. Teachers & Writers Collaborative thanks the students,
teachers, administrators, and staff of all our partners on this project.